OTHER BOOKS IN THE SERIES

by Schiffer Publishing Ltd.

The Kaiser's Army in Color: Uniforms of the Imperial German Army as Illustrated by Carl Becker 1890-1910

Uniforms of Imperial and Soviet Russia in Color: As Illustrated by Herbert Knötel, dj. 1907-1946

British Army Uniforms in Color: As Illustrated by John McNeill, Ernest Ibbetson, Edgar A. Holloway, and Harry Payne c.1908-1919

The Ackermann Military Prints: Uniforms of the British and Indian Armies 1840-1855

Queen Victoria's Army in Color: The British Military Paintings of Orlando Norie

IN THE SERVICE OF THE KAISER

Uniforms & Equipment of the World War I German Soldier
as Painted by Soldier-Artist Friedrich Ludwig Scharf

Charles Woolley

Schiffer Military History
Atglen, PA

Acknowledgements

Peter Harrington and Bob Kenny from the Anne S.K. Brown Military Collection, faithful Nancy with the magic fingers, and Bob Biondi for allowing me to drift off once again in another direction. My deepest thanks.

Book design by Robert Biondi.

Printed in China.
ISBN: 0-7643-1981-7

For the largest selection of fine reference books on this and related subjects, please visit our website – **www.schifferbooks.com** – or call for a free catalog.

We are always looking for people to write books on new and related subjects. If you have an idea for a book, please contact us at the address below.

Published by Schiffer Publishing Ltd.	In Europe, Schiffer books are distributed by:
4880 Lower Valley Road	Bushwood Books
Atglen, PA 19310	6 Marksbury Ave.
Phone: (610) 593-1777	Kew Gardens
FAX: (610) 593-2002	Surrey TW9 4JF
E-mail: Info@schifferbooks.com.	England
Visit our web site at: www.schifferbooks.com	Phone: 44 (0)20 8392-8585
Please write for a free catalog.	FAX: 44 (0)20 8392-9876
This book may be purchased from the publisher.	E-mail: info@Bushwoodbooks.co.uk.
Please include $3.95 postage.	Free postage in the UK. Europe: air mail at cost.
Try your bookstore first.	Try your bookstore first.

CONTENTS

Introduction 7

Chapter 1   The Artist 8

Chapter 2   The Sketchbook 10

Chapter 3   "Buntes Tuch" or "Colorful Cloth" 18

Chapter 4   "Zweierlei Tuch" or "Two Kinds of Cloth" 26

INTRODUCTION

If one were to undertake an in-depth study of the uniforms worn by the German Imperial Army during the First Great War period, the researcher would find many published sources on the subject, some accurate, some not. Photographs are available in abundance and are unquestionably accurate, but at the same time misleading as to tonal and color quality. The prints made from film available in 1914-1918 often had drastically changed appearances of color or tone; for instance, yellow would often appear on a photographic print as black. Many printed references in color were produced contemporarily by publishers like Verlag von Moritz Ruhl of Leipzig, which were schematic in format, with side views drawn up of caps, uniforms and epaulets, which were on occasion incorrect. *Oberleutnant Freiheer* v.d. Osten-Sachen employed the military painter Paul Casberg to illustrate *Deutschlands Armee in feldgrauer* that he executed schematically, as well as in full figure form. Both are well painted, but are not representative of the appearance of men at the front. Otto Weiss produced *Feldgrau in Krieg und Frieden* which illustrated the 1915 uniform regulations as laid down by the *Allerhöchsten Kabinettsordre* von 21, September 1915. Again, this was presented in a schematic format and was painfully correct by regulation, but not in the reality of active service. The work of contemporary artists whose feel and understanding of the correct colors, coupled with period photographs showing how the uniforms were actually worn at the front, have to be the closest to authenticity that can be found. The pictures that follow are one dedicated man's conscious artistic effort toward that end, painted by a serving soldier who had been there.

CHAPTER ONE

THE ARTIST

On the leap year day of February 29, 1884, a son was born to Maria and Friedrich Christian Scharf. The infant, Friedrich Ludwig Scharf, entered a family world filled with music. His father, a professional musician, particularly enjoyed playing military marches and airs as well as classical music, while his mother taught voice and piano. Ludwig, at an early age, found that drawing came to him more easily than music, and as a result he pursued an education in the field of art at the famous Münster School of Art.

Later, the military life, as well as art, appealed to Scharf, and upon leaving Münster and the formal part of his education behind, he volunteered for service with the *Grossherzoglich Mecklenburg-ischen Jäger Bataillion Nr.14* in Colmar. In 1913, while on maneuvers with his regiment near the French border, he met, fell in love with, and married Elise Quenzer from the town of Wölchingen, a marriage that lasted for fifty-two years. He quickly rose through the non-commissioned ranks being named in 1915 the "*bataillion Fahnentrager*", or flagbearer, and by 1918 he was promoted to *Offizierstellvertrater* and *Kompanieführer* of the 8. *Kompanie*, 1. *Jäger* Regiment.

In 1914, at the outbreak of the Great War, Ludwig and Elise Scharf were living in Heidelberg from where Ludwig's unit was quickly mobilized and dispatched to the Eastern, or Russian front. There, and later in Finland, Scharf served most of his wartime duty. As an NCO he was highly thought of by his men for whose welfare he always showed his first concern. He was wounded in late 1914, rapidly recovered, and rejoined his unit at the front for the balance of the hostilities. When the war ended, Ludwig found himself, like so many professional soldiers, out of work and with no immediate future in view. With a family to support, he reluctantly became a trainee for a financial organization, but quickly found the dullness

and limitations of office work were not for the artist in him. Since leaving art school, he had continually practiced his first passion, painting, and when he found time during his military service, he sketched and recorded in watercolors the every day army life that surrounded him.

By 1923, living in Wölchingen, Baden, he decided to turn his hand to work as a freelance artist. In 1925 one of his first known published efforts, the artwork for *Frankischer Heimatkalender für das Jahr 1925*, was published by Deutscher Verlag in Würzberg, and was followed shortly thereafter by illustrations for the 400th Jubilee of the "Bauernkrieges" or Peasants War, entitled *Bauer mit Fahne*, or Peasants with Flags. During this early period of his chosen work, he became acquainted with many other German artists who were producing all manner of illustrations relating to military subjects. Herbert Knötel *der junger*, following in his father Richard's footsteps, Paul Pietsch, Oscar Merte, Georg Schäfer, Erich Döbrich-

Left: Feldwebel Ludwig Scharf, pre-1910. Right: Ludwig Scharf prior to his death in 1965.

Steglitz, Anton Hoffmann and Carl Becker were all active military artists in the 1920s and 1930s.

Published in the late 1920s for consumption by patriotic minded veterans of the Great War were many large format oversized books extolling the bravery and past history of many German regiments, and, more broadly, specific branches of the service. Preparation for these volumes required not only photographs, but also illustrations rendered by contemporary artists both in pen and ink and painted in color. The aforementioned artists were quick to respond to this call, including Ludwig Scharf who created a series entitled, *Infanterie und Kavallerie Fahen und Standarten*, meticulously drawn flags for the two-volume *Das Deutschen Soldatenbuch* by Major F.F. Deiss and published in 1928 by Vaterländischer Verlag in Berlin.

Some of the military painters joined forces to produce and publish various books and series of historical and accurate uniform plates, "Das Kasket," *Handdruck zur Geschichte Der Militärischen Tracht* being one example that, unfortunately, after two years and one hundred thirty-seven published plates, was discontinued. Scharf published at least five series of his own uniform paintings; namely, *Zweierli Tuch, Buntes Tuch, Das Fürstbischöflich Muntsterische Militar in 18. Jahrhundert, Die Kurpfalz-Bayrische Armee 1785*, and *Aus einem alten preuss. Exerzier-Reglement un 1700*. Knötel continued his father's massive *Uniformendunde* plate series and updated the famous reference book *Handbuch der Uniformkunde*.

Ludwig loved to paint soldiers from all periods of history, but only examples of his uniform illustrations of the twentieth century are depicted in this book and are taken from the *Zweierlie Tuch*, or "Two Kinds of Cloth" and *Buntes Tuch*, or "Colorful Cloth" series, plus Scharf's actual sketchbook. Scharf was an avid student of all styles of military costume, with his scholarly curiosity taking his work from the Peasants War of 1425 through the *Reichswehr* of the 1930s. Painting in watercolor and producing hand-colored linoleum block prints, Ludwig's style was unique and sometimes slightly crude in an almost caricature form. The background seen in many of his First War works reflects the unmistakable landscapes he witnessed during his service in Russia and Finland as part of the German Baltic Division. This division, under *General* von der Goltz, reinforced the Finn's led by General Mannerheim which defeated the Red Forces on 28-29 April 1918 at Viborg. This is most evident in drawings in one of Scharf's sketchbooks to be described in the following chapter.

Scharf, second from the right, as "Bataillion Fahnentrager" 1915.

Scharf had a fondness for the cavalry and as conditions at the Eastern front required the presence of many of the mounted regiments, his sketchbook depicts the variations of *Husaren, Ulanen, Dragoner* and *Kürassier* uniforms worn on campaign.

The Second World War heavily curtailed Ludwig's artistic work, and after the war there was little call for military drawings. To survive, he turned to the design of hand-decorated china and even tried his skill at designing patterns to be stitched by hand to peasant-style blouses for the export trade. As his economic circumstances improved, he returned to painting military subjects, continuing to do so until his death on 27 October 1965 at the age of eighty-one. Ludwig Scharf left a definite mark among the military artists of his time, painting in a style unique to him, always done with an accurate eye for detail and even a little humor toward many of the subjects he depicted.

CHAPTER TWO

THE SKETCHBOOK

We are fortunate that one of Scharf's sketchbooks survives in the holdings of the vast Anne S.K. Brown Military Collection at Brown University, Providence, Rhode Island. Viewing an artist's preliminary sketches gives the student of his work another degree of insight into the man's creativity and the details that he found interesting while contemplating a finished work. Small drawings of uniform details can be seen in these pages of sketches, details which may not be obvious in a finished painting, but which never-the-less were important to the artist to ensure that his depiction was correct and accurate.

This sketchbook itself is of an unusual size, 13"x15", large, when we think of other examples encountered which normally are 8"x12" and often smaller. The book contains thirty pages of artist quality paper bound with marbleized cardboard covers and finished on the back spine with imitation leather cloth. The majority of Scharf's entries were done in black pen and ink, although there are several pages containing sketches finished in watercolors. Many pages without illustrations contain handwritten information about specific units, mostly cavalry, outlining uniform variations, the size of units, names of officers, divisions to which they were attached and where and at what date they fought. Fourteen illustrated pages have been selected for inclusion here to give the reader the opportunity to see how Scharf compiled data for later paintings.

Husaren Regiment Nr. 11 (Top); and Kürassier Regiment Nr. 8 (Bottom)

Husaren Regiment Nr. 11; Dragoner Regiment Nr. 19 (Top); Husaren Regiment Nr. 11 (Bottom)

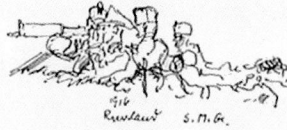

Husaren Regiment Nr. 11 and a Feldgeistlicher, or Chaplain (Top); Husaren Regiment Nr. 11 (Bottom)

Reserve Husaren Regiment Nr. 8, Dragoner Regiment Nr. 19, Husaren Regiment Nr. 11 (Top); nineteenth century French Cavalry Regiment, Husaren Regiment Nr. 11 (Bottom)

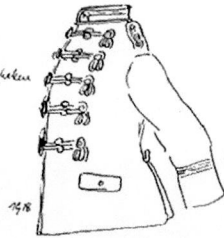

Preussen Reserve Husaren Regiment Nr. 8 (Top); Kürassier Regiment Nr. 4 (Bottom)

Württembergische Schneeschuh Komp. Nr. 1 (Top); Württembergische Gebirgs. Bataillion, 6 Kompanie (Bottom)

Württembergische Sanitorsoffizier (Top)/reserve Husaren Regiment Nr. 8, 3. Escadr. In the Ukraine 1918 (Bottom)

CHAPTER THREE

"BUNTES TUCH" OR "COLORFUL CLOTH"

Scharf's *Buntes Tuch* was originally produced as a series of loose individual plates, the printing starting at Münster in 1935 and continuing through 1939 or 1940. The style used in this series was greatly different than that in Scharf's larger work *Zweirlei Tuch*, or "Two Kinds of Cloth." Most of the paintings were watercolors instead of the rather coarse linoleum hand-colored block prints normally associated with the artist's work. Scharf's paintings for *Buntes Tuch* focused more on the uniforms of the army of Friedrich the Great and uniforms of many nationalities from the period of the Napoleonic Wars, but the series did contain seven paintings of uniforms from the twentieth century that are unusual and included here.

Landsturm-Jnf·Batl·
Heidelberg
Vize-Feldw.
Winter 1914/15

L·SCHARF

A Vizefeldwebel of the Landsturm-Infanterie-Bataillion-Heidelberg. The subject is depicted wearing a brass-trimmed M60/97 tschako with the Baden winged griffin front plate and red and yellow feldzeichen. Of interest is the feldgrau cape with Landsturm collar insignia, brown ledergamash, or leather legwraps, and laced low-quarter boots.

Würrttembergisches Gebirgs-Batl.
Januar 1916
Vizefeldwebel

234

LUDWIG·SCHARF

A Vizefeldwebel of the Württembergisches Gebirgs-Bataillion in winter mountain equipment. Scharf painted the central figure armed with a Kar. 98a and a M 98ab bayonet and wearing the unique uniform of mountain troops, a mütze, or ski cap with folding earflaps, a unique jacket, warm goat hair stockings, cleated mountain boots and mountain trousers, or Gebirghosen which are all clearly shown. Of special note are the large muff or hand warmer, suspended around the subject's neck, snow goggles, map case with an isinglass cover, and the horizontal "S" for ski troops on the collar of the uniform jacket.

Abzeichen
a. linken
Unter=
arm

Flammenwerfer-
Truppführer.
Garde-Reserve
Pionier-Regt.
1916/1917

Flammenwerfer-Truppenführer from the Garde-Reserve-Pionier-Regiment in full field gear. Notable are the M 16 Stahlhelm, Gew. 98, double feldflaske canteens, breadbag, large sack strapped to the field pack, leather enforced combat trousers, or hosen, legwraps, or wickelgamaschen, mountain boots, pionier long-handled shovel and the totenkopf insignia worn on the left lower arm. The long stick held by the subject with a kerosene soaked rag on its end was used to start or ignite the flammenwerfer. This is a detail not noted before.

Kraft-Rad-Abt.
741 Nazareth.
Unteroffizier
1917

L·SCHARF

An Unteroffizier of Kraft-Rad-Abteilung 741 is depicted wearing the summer weight khaki cotton uniform, khaki mütze, and brown leather equipment. Scharf's eye for detail is shown in his depiction of a Radfahrer Gewehr 98 with the sling side-attached and a turned down bolt leaning on the wall. These rare rifles were designed for and issued to bicycle troops so that they could carry their rifles slung on their backs while riding. It is interesting that the Gew. 98 was modified, rather than issuing the Kar. 98a to the Radahrer troops which would have worked just as well.

1. Westfäl. Reichswehr
Schützen-Regt. № 13
Minenwerfer Komp.
Sept. 1919

This painting of the 1. Westfälische-Reichswehr Schützen-Regiment No. 13 contains many interesting details. The man is attached to the Minenwerfer (Mortar) Kompanie as indicated by the letters "MW" on the left sleeve and the shoulder straps. The special braided fangschnur of the Westfälisher Verbande is woven from green, white and black cords in the style of the Imperial shooting award, or Schützenschnur. The rosette is cloverleaf-shaped and attached to it is a silver heraldic-style horse and two award acorns below in green. On the left arm of the M 1915 bluse is the old army, Alte Armee, shield insignia of the Münster Infanterie-Rgt. Herworth von Bittenfeld (1. Westfälische) Nr. 13 and part of the VII Armee Korps of the Kaiser's army. Below the shield is a chevron most commonly seen on Freikorps uniforms, this example in the colors of Westphalia. On the epaulet is an added ribbon printed in the tri-color black, white and red of the loyal Reichswehr forces. Armed with a Kar. 98a, the balance of his equipment is also all of World War I vintage.

1939   *L.SCHARF*

Schellenbaum·der·Landes-Polizei,
     Übernommen·vom·Jnf·Regt·№79

211

The Schellenbaum, or "Jingling Johnnie" of the National police attached to Infanterie Regiment Nr. 79, the first three "bataillions" which were garrisoned in Münster where Scharf painted a great deal of his work. The painting is dated 1939 and shows no evidence of Halkenkrautz, or swastika insignia on the Schellenbaum. Only the police-style eagle is visible on the banner below the spread eagle on its top. Without question, the Nazi breast eagle, or Hoheitsabzeichen was worn on the right chest of the man's parade waffenrock. This is an unusually late period subject to be illustrated by the artist.

Russland 1914
5. Schützen Regt.
Standort: Radom 14·A·K·
Unteroffizier

Scharf's exposure to the Russians in the early stages of the war left a lasting impression on him and he painted this one example of a rifleman of the 5th Rifle Regiment. The fleece cap is normally worn in winter weather in lieu of the visored service cap. This soldier is dressed in the 1907 light olive green service dress, a leather waist belt with a brass buckle embossed with the Russian double-headed eagle, and double thirty-round ammunition pouches. On his right side, handle down, is a Linnemann entrenching tool, a one-sixth part of a tent and tent pole, and over the shoulder, horseshoe-fashion, is his rolled greatcoat and extra boots, and completing his personal equipment is an oval copper mess tin. His weapon is the Mosin-Nagant M 1891 standard infantry five-shot rifle with the cruciform-section M 1891 bayonet which was always in the fixed position when the troops were at the front, the scabbards being left in depots at the rear.

"ZWEIERLEI TUCH" OR "TWO KINDS OF CLOTH"

T his series was produced in a larger format than that of *Buntes Tuch* and contained approximately one hundred-forty plates. Ninety-two are included in this book, the balance being made up of uniforms from earlier periods. The plates were issued over several years, and it is difficult to find a complete set, although the Anne S.K. Brown Military Collection has both the *Zweierlei Tuch* and *Buntes Tuch* in their entirety, which took them some twenty years to complete with assistance from book and print sellers throughout Europe. The majority of this work is in the linoleum-block style, with a few watercolors thrown in for variety.

ZWEIERLEI TUCH

Original-Linolschnitte

zur

Geschichte der Uniformen

Ludwig Scharf, Kunstmaler, Münster-Westfalen

BL.7

LUDWIG·SCHARF

A trooper of the mounted 5. Kompanie of the III. See-Bataillion stationed at Kiautschou, China, 1911 wears the tan tropical uniform issued to Naval and Colonial troops. Shoulder boards with a yellow crown over crossed anchors over "III" are in evidence. Over his shoulder is the "Bandolier mit Patronentäschchen fur berittene Mannschoften des ostasiatischen Reiter-Regiments." This bandolier held five leather pouches and was supplemented with four waist pouches, two left and two right. The Gew. 98 is carried in a brown leather boot to which is attached a pouch for spare horseshoes. A tropical helmet of cork covered in tan cotton material was issued to the See-Bataillions with a naval-style tschako plate of a colonial eagle clutching an anchor in his talons.

Zweierlei Tuch"

A Wachtmeister, or patrolman, of the mounted Landespolizes, Southwest Africa, 1914. The filzhut, or felt hat Scharf depicts is different in color – tan, brown, and without the colored border on the rim – than the light grey hats normally seen worn by other troops in Southwest Africa. The khaki feldrock, or tropenuniform has a green collar with two rank pips and green shoulder boards. The facings color for the regular troops in "Südwestafrika" were blue. This Wachtmeister is armed with a Kar. 98a and is seated on a regulation issue army saddle.

A trooper of the Südafrikanisches-Freikorps, 1914-1915. Scharf illustrates a fully equipped rider of the Schutztruppe in Deutsche-Südwestafrika. The blue collar and cuff facings on the corduroy tropical uniform are the color for troops assigned to Southwest Africa. The "Patronengurtels 94" with the twelve individual pouches is evident, as is the Gew. 98 in its brown leather boot.

Prussian staff and general officers, 1914-1916. The saluting captain on the General Staff has triple rose-pink stripes on his trousers and the same colored piping on his tunic. This color was unique to General Staff officers. The general in the background wears a feldgrauer mantel M 1915, or einheitsmantel economy model, under which he wears a feldbluse, which with the mantel, is piped in red. The next general wears the earlier style walking out, or ausrück uniform and a light grey mantel with a dark blue collar with a dress binde, or belt to complete the outfit. The third general wears an officer's raincoat over his feldbluse.

Prussian Generals, 1914-1916. The general on the left is dressed in a standard walking out uniform and is equipped with 08 Fernglas binoculars, map case, holstered pistol and Lionhead officer's sword with the war-time black painted scabbard. The general on the right wears a variation of the general officer's feldbluse, with general's collar tabs. The feldbluse worn by other generals have been observed with no breast pockets and plain darker green collars. The leather feldbinde, or belt worn with a dress bayonet is an interesting detail.

Infanterie Regiment von Courbière (2. Posen.) Nr. 19 formed in 1813 in Görlitz. In this painting Scharf shows two officers, one of whom is the adjutant, and an NCO, and in full equipment, a signaler, as indicated by the crossed flags on his right sleeve. The artist brings to our attention that the field belts and the adjutant's sash are made of grey material other than metallic braid seen in peacetime. The adjutant carries an officer's ID 89 sword.

Scharf departs from the hand-colored linoleum-block process for a pencil and watercolor sketch of a 1914 Landsturmer Prussian from the 1. Ers. Btl. Landwehr-Infanterie Regiment Nr. 12 1. Kompanie. Armed with an M 88 commission rifle and a Seitengewehr M 71 brass-hilted bayonet, this Prussian wears a tschako with field cover and the old style black overcoat or mantel with black Landsturm shoulder straps and red collar patches. This painting depicts the bleak winter weather conditions encountered on the Eastern front.

Members of Landsturm-Pionier-Kompanie 9, October 1914. The Gefreiter on the left is wearing the old style pre-1910 black trousers and blue Litewka, M 1893, with shoulder straps of black coarsely woven material with the unit designation worn on the collar. His feldmütze is of the pre-1910 blue color, with a black band designating pionier-truppen and his rifle is an outdated Gew. 88 as provided to Landsturm and second line troops. The Feldwebel-Leutnant wears the M 1910 uniform with NCO tressing on the collar, an NCO sword, canteen, breadbag, pistol, and binocular case suspended from an enlisted model belt.

The Preussen Landsturm VII. 10 soldier on the left is wearing the M 1893 Litewka, black, red piped trousers, Patronentasche 95 pouches, and Seitengewehr 71 and Gew. 88 for weapons. The tschako is the M 1860 alter Art fur Landsturm, or the old model for Landsturm with the Landsturm plate on the front. The Ostpreussischer-Landsturm on the right is wearing the M 1910 tunic with no shoulder straps, a Prussian Jäger tschako and the same field equipment as the man on the left.

Prussian Landsturm-Feldartillerie, 1914. The NCO on the left wears a light grey M 1903 Litewka with shoulder straps of red coarse material and a grey Landsturm visor cap with a large Landsturm cross and Prussian cockade. The Wachmeister on the right wears a standard Foot Artillery M 1910 waffenrock and an oilcloth visor cap of the Landsturm style. Both men carry nickel finished Dovehead artillery swords. Note the white leather belt and crossbelt on the man on the right.

LUDWIG·SCHARF

Ostpreussischer-Landsturm on the Eastern front, 1914. These two Landsturmers are wearing Litewkas M 1893 and M 1903, both equipped with breadbags of white canvas, canteens slung from the beadbag straps, M 1860 tschakos, one, strangely shown, without a frontplate, Gew. 88 rifles and M 71 bayonets.

A Musketier from Infanterie Regiment "Harworth von Bittenfeld" (1. Westfälisches) Nr. 13 on the advance in full field gear. Note the blue piping on his shoulder straps for the VII Armee Korps of which the 13th was part. In this painting Scharf returns to a softer style of pencil and watercolor.

Two members of the Feldgendarmerie of the 14. Armee Korps, August 1914. Both are wearing the distinctive green Feldgendarmerie model tunic; the man on the left has Swedish cuffs and collar litzen, the NCO on the right has Polish cuffs and no litzen. They wear the gorgets of their Korps, indicated by the Roman numeral XIV and their man number in Arabic numerals, 79 and 80, and in each corner, the Prussian eagle. Their "Dragoner" style helmets bear field covers and retain the brass chinscales or "Schuppenketten." The swords illustrated appear to be the same as issued to the Train-Bataillionen.

Prussian Oberzahlmeister and Trainfahrer, 1914. The senior paymaster on the left wears an M 1910 tunic with dark blue collar tabs and trim on his shoulder straps; the same color appears on the band of his visor cap which is worn with a chinstrap. The uniform piping is white. The Trainfahrer is from the Truppe assigned to the 2. Ober-Alsässisches Infanterie Regiment Nr. 171, and also wears the M 1910 tunic, reinforced mounted troop trousers and mounted troop high boots and spurs. The Train colors of light blue are worn on an armband attached in the center of the left upper arm. The Schurmütze, or visor cap, M 1912 seen here is of the style worn by many of the mobilized troops of the period.

Prussian Musicians, 1914. The drawing on the left portrays the Bataillion Drum Major of Grenadier-Regiment König Wilhelm I (2. Westpreussisches) Nr. 7. He is in full field gear armed with a pistol and an NCO sword. The epaulets of his M 1910 tunic bear the cipher of Wilhelm I, as well as the yellow and red litzen of the regiment. The drum major's "Schwalbennester" shoulder badges are woven gold wire and carry the extra lower fringe befitting his rank. While not performing his musical duties, he serves as a signaler as shown by the crossed flags on his right sleeve. The Musikmeister on the right is from the Colberg-Grenadier-Regiment Graf Gneisenau (2. Pommersches) Nr. 9. Note the special epaulet with the lyre insignia of a Musikmeister, and silver fringed Schwalbennesters denoting his position.

Scharf chooses to illustrate the unusual subject of a mounted mail carrier of the Kaiserlich Deutsche Feldpost in the M 1914 feldgrau uniform. The same style uniform was first introduced as the M 1907, but the tunic and cap were in dark blue and the riding breeches in black. The insignia on the shoulder straps is in the shape of a hunting horn, or "posthorn," and the cap insignia is a Kaiserlichen Adler, or eagle over the posthorn and lightning bolts. A dark blue band surrounds his visor cap which is of the M 1907 style, but in feldgrau. The horse furniture is of army issue and a train model sword hangs from the rear of the saddle.

Feldgeistliche, or field clergymen wore a variety of feldgrau uniforms, but this painting is most unusual as it depicts a Franciscan monk, complete with brown monk's robes, on duty with Herresgruppe von Falkenhausen, 1915. The band on his visor cap is purple which was the distinctive color for clergymen, but the insignia on this cap did not include the cross which was normally worn by members of the clergy.

Signal troops of Ersatz-Infanterie-Regiment Nr. 29, November 1916. This regiment was formed from units of the 7. Badisches Infanterie Regiment Nr. 142. The first and second bataillions were from Baden; the third were Prussians. Scharf comments on the men's lack of signaler badges or insignia. The signal flags were blue, red and white. The equipment shown is standard issue for infantrymen, along with the Fernglas 08 binoculars and the flashlight around the neck of the man in the center.

LUDWIG·SHARF

Uniforms changed from 1914 through 1917 for soldiers of "Preussen Infanterie Regiment 'Frhr. Von Sparr' (3. Westf.) Nr. 16." In 1914 the M 1894 mantel or overcoat was in use with red collar patches and pre-1910 blue epaulets with chain-stitched red numerals. The man on the left has a cloth bandolier, or Tragegurt fur Patronen M 1907 around his shoulders and brown M 09 Patronentasche on his belt. On his Gew. 98 is what appears to be a steel-hilted ersatz bayonet. The man on the right wears an M 15 bluse, black M 09 Patronentasche on his belt, suspended by a breadbag strap and a gas mask carried in a canvas pouch with the numeral "2" on its end. By 1917 most leather equipment was being issued dyed black, rather than the brown of earlier issue.

In this watercolor, Scharf illustrates three different styles of the uniform of "Preussen Reserve Infanterie Regiment Nr. 81. The Hauptmann on the left wears the officer's feldbluse with epaulets, heavy twill breeches with reinforced knees, riding boots with spurs and is armed with a holstered P. 08 and a dress bayonet on his left hip. The Musketier in the center wears his covered pickelhaube without the spike and is dressed for combat. The trusty Feldwebel wears his M 1910 waffenrock with his rank chevrons on his sleeve and his "duty" book tucked in front ready to take the name of any defaulter. An ID 89 sword and a P. 08 in a brown holster make up his armament.

A Musketier from the Preussen Infanterie Regiment Graf Dönhoff (7. Ostpreussisches) Nr. 44, as he looked in 1917 is painted by Scharf wearing an M 1910 tunic with a blue fabric band covering the regimental numbers on his epaulets. Blue bands designated the 1. Bataillion, red the II. Bataillion, and gold the III. Bataillion. The spike has been removed from his pickelhaube indicating service at the front lines, as does the gas mask in its canvas bag slung on his waistbelt. His leather equipment is black. The Landsturmer is shown in a feldgrau Litewka, with blue coarsely woven shoulder straps and the Number "6" chainstitched on them. He wears the old pattern side-laced low boot or schnürschuh and carries an M 71 bayonet. The date depicted was 1914.

An Offizierstellvertrater and a private of a "Minenwerfer Kompagnie" from the Preussen Infanterie Regiment "Graf Schwerin" (3. Pommersches) Nr. 14. The Offizierstellvertrater wears an M 15 bluse, the shoulder straps of which have tressing and the regimental numbers. He is equipped with riding breeches, cavalry-style boots, M 16 Stahlhelm, an open buckle cavalry belt, brown holster for the P. 08, and a brown utility or map case. Both men wear a grenade insignia on the left arm, one in grey metal and the other in gold embroidery. They are shown as they looked in 1916.

Supply and provision troops in 1916. Proviantamts und Feldmagazinbeamte, or Food and Warehouse inspectors in the M 1915 feldbluse with blue identifying colors on their caps and yellow shoulder boards. A Feld-Backmeister is on the left and an Unterinspektor is on the right.

A Prussian Landsturm sentry on duty in "Bukarest," Rumania, winter 1917. For warmth, he has been issued the feldgrauer mantel or overcoat M 1915 and heavy wool mittens. Note the sentry box painted in black, white and red stripes, the Prussian national colors.

Scharf depicts a rather scruffy looking Prussian staff doctor assigned to a reserve component of Infanterie Regiment Nr. 81. The medical branch collar litzen are on his M 15 bluse and interestingly, he is painted wearing an enlisted man's cavalry riding breeches with infantry-style boots with spurs and a dress bayonet with trodel.

"Zweierlei Tuch"

LUDWIG·SCHARF

A Musketier and an Unteroffizier from a Brandenburg regiment pause for a break in the trench fighting.
They are wearing the protective grabenhose, or trench trousers over their regular trousers and tucked
into their boots. Although the date is 1917, they are dressed in the M 1910 tunic with Brandenburg cuffs
which were starting to look rather shabby. The Musketier on the left is still equipped with black
Patronentasche M 95 cartridge boxes which were issued originally with the Gew. 88. The pipe smoking
Unteroffizier is ready for action, fully equipped and loaded with extra ammunition.

*Scharf enjoyed painting subjects from Infanterie Regiment Herwarth von Bittenfeld (1. Westälisches)
Nr. 13, as proven by this illustration. In 1917 Sturmtruppen were in use and equipped as is shown by
the man on the right. Pionier long-handled shovels, mountain boots, legwraps, leather reinforced combat
trousers, M 16 helmets and assault packs made up much of the stormtrooper's equipment. The man on
the left would have been in a more static position as he is equipped with the articulated trench body
armor and the steel brow plate affixed to his M 16 helmet. Note he is wearing his feldmütze under his
helmet and brow plate possibly to relieve the pressure caused by the weight of the two items.*

A trench sentry from 5. Westfälisches Infanterie Regiment Nr. 53 stares out over no-man's-land. His M 16 helmet is camouflaged, his tunic is an M 15 bearing the red crown cipher insignia of I.R. 53 on the shoulder straps, with the standard infantry equipment making up the remainder of his gear. Note the spool of telephone communication wire resting on the edge of the trench.

Scharf's interest in Münster regiments, most likely because he lived there, is evident in this painting of a member of Fusilier Regiment General Ludendorff (Niederrheinisches) Nr. 39. Equipped with an M 16 helmet, Gew. 98 and all the other standard field gear, including a gas mask in its metal carrier around his neck at the ready, this determined Musketier is on his way to the trenches.

Two Grenadiere from Sturm Bataillion Nr. III display the dress and equipment of stormtroopers as seen in 1917. Clearly shown are the grenades and grenade bags made from sandbag sacking, reinforced combat trousers, a trench knife, a pioniere long-handled shovel, double canteens, a gas mask in its canvas carrier, and Kar. 98a rifles.

Armor was essential for protection of lookouts and sentries in the trenches in 1917. Here Scharf has painted a sentry taking advantage of two protective Sappenpanzer M 1916-1917 set at angles to one another, and of the sentinel's body armor worn over his back. This body armor was made of silicon-nickel steel and resisted standard rifle ammunition at sixty yards, but armor piercing ammunition would penetrate up to three hundred yards. The body armor was designed to be worn either front or back and Ludendorff requested that the armor be issued to static forward stationed troops noting that it should be used "especially as a protection for the back."

A Jäger from Reserve-Jäger Bataillion Nr. 8 is painted firing his Gew. 98 from a firing step in the trench. On his left is a mirror flexibly mounted on a pole which can be elevated into an upright position in order that the area forward of the trench could be safely observed. The man must feel secure in his position as he has discarded his helmet for a mütze with a dark green band and piping as worn by the Jäger troops.

Another trench scene illustrates an Offizierstellvertrater and a Musketier of Infanterie Regiment Generalfeldmarschell von Hindenburg (2. Masurisches) Nr. 147 awaiting an allied attack. The NCO is dressed in the M 15 feldbluse and his trousers, without piping, are made of the same material as the bluse. The rifleman wears the M 1910 waffenrock and grey trousers with a red stripe. The shoulder straps for I.R. 147 were edged in blue and bore the regimental numbers chainstitched in red.

A machine gunner, or M.G. Schütze opens a camouflaged Patronenkaste or ammunition box for his MG 08 machine gun which is also camouflaged in the style of the stahlhelms of the same 1918 period. The red band on his mütze has been covered by a grey strap to reduce its visibility to the enemy. The machine gunners badge, or abzeichen on his sleeve is not, as would be normally seen, mounted on feldgrau material and surrounded by a metal oval in the shape of an endless belt of ammunition. This could have been a possible field modification. Whatever its origin, it was mounted over a black chevron on the left sleeve. As were most machine gun troops, he is armed with an M 96 Mauser in its wooden holster/shoulder stock, as well as with a Seitengewehr 98/05, the most widely issued German bayonet of World War I. He also has a flexibly mounted tilting trench mirror to observe conditions beyond the barbed wire.

Here we see a rather neatly dressed, that is for a tank crew member, NCO of 2. Reserve Kompanie Pionier Bataillion Nr. 26, Schwere Panzerwagen Abteilung Grandenz, standing before a camouflaged A7V Sturm-Panzerkraftwagen. In contrast to the insignia shown in the previous painting, this man wears the M. G. Scharfeshutzen badge with the cloth background, machine gun, and metal oval. His shoulder straps are marked with a red "K" for Kraftfahr and 26 on his M 15 bluse. Ledergamasche and laced boots replace the normal marching boots for this tanker.

Little evidence is available regarding the uniforms worn on the Palestine front in 1918. In this picture Scharf portrays two Musketiere of 1. Masurisches Infanterie Regiment Nr. 146 while on duty on that front. They are dressed in the khakibluse M 17 and are equipped with khakimütze, also M 17. The illustration does not clearly show the attachment of the neck protection sun shields. In reality they were attached onto the two buttons which held the chinstrap and were tied in the rear by a cord which was connected to the cap itself. The khakibluse M 17 actually had six detachable buttons painted in a sand brown color, removable shoulder straps and two lower patch pockets. The man on the right carries an assault pack, pionier shovel, a Seitengewehr M 98/05 and a breadbag of rust-colored material. He is equipped like Western front sturmtruppen minus the grenade bags.

Telegraph troops in the field, 1918. On the left a Gefreiter from Fernsprech-Abteilung 121 relays information from the front while the man on the right from Nachrichten Ersatz Abteilung Nr. 18 feeds him the necessary communication wire. The man on the right wears the red "T" for telegraph troops on his shoulder straps and the designation of Fernsprech Abteilung 18 in a red rectangle on his left sleeve.

On the left Scharf depicts Musketier Frank from the Garnison Kompagnie in the uniform of Jäger-Bataillion Nr. 14. These limited duty troops were issued all models of rifles and bayonets and variations of uniforms. Musketier Frank has been issued a Jäger bluse with litzen, collar insignia and grey infantry trousers with a red stripe. The litzen on the collar is unusual as it was normally worn only by the 14th and Garde-Jäger Bataillion. The NCO on the right from Infanterie Regiment Nr. 171 appears as he would have looked in 1918 wearing a pickelhaube with field cover, not a steel helmet, a 1910 tunic with trousers with green Jäger stripes. So much for conformity in the Imperial army.

The fall of 1914 on the Eastern front saw troopers of Kürassier Regiment von Driesen (Westfälisches) Nr. 4 wearing M 1910 Koller-style tunics, riding breeches and tall brown mounted troop boots, or Kavalleriestiefel, with spurs. The man on the right is equipped with an M 1889/94 Kürassier helmet with a field cover, cavalry-style belt and brown leather "Y" straps supporting M 1911 Patronentaschen. The feldmütze for the 4th worn by the trooper on the left has the identical piping and band colors as was used by the Garde du Corps.

An Unteroffizier and Kürassier on the attack 1914-1916 on the Russian front. They both wear the distinctive Koller-style tunic unique to Kürassier units, the Leib Kürassier Regiment, Grosser Kurfüst, (Schlesisches) Nr. 1 uniforms bore white and black piping and a red "WR" cipher and crown on their shoulder straps. The heavy Kürassier brass-hilted sword and the M 1893 Stahlrohrlanze are clearly shown, the lance being carried without its pennant which could be affixed to the buttons on the tip.

Heavily armed light cavalry on the Eastern front. Troopers of Westfälisches Dragoner Regiment Nr. 7 are painted as they appeared in 1914. The 7th was one of three Dragoner Regiments which had pink piping on its uniforms. Of interest is the rust-colored zeltbahn or shelter-half rolled and worn over the shoulder. Steel lances, Kar. 98a carbines, and M 1893 helm für Berittene with their grey cotton field covers complete the picture.

A trooper from the Kurmärkisches Dragoner Regiment Nr. 14 is portrayed as he looked in 1915. Uniforms of the 14th carried white piping with the regimental number in red chainstitched to the shoulder straps. His sword is a Kavallerie Degan M 89 with the Prussian eagle engraved on the plated guard. Stahlrohrlanze M 93, Kar. 98a, pickelhaube M 93 and Patronentasche M 11 cartridge boxes round out his armament and equipment.

A Hussar from Husaren-Regiment von Zieten (Brandenburgisches) Nr. 3 wearing the grey wartime uniform which was in stark contrast to the bright red atilla worn before the introduction of feldgrau. Over the black fur of his pelzmütze, the grey field cover is worn with a black and white feldzeichen affixed to the front. The Kar. 98a is carried in a brown scabbard on the left side of the saddle and a KD 89 sword on the right side; the steel lance and horse furniture are standard light cavalry issue.

The Ersatz Eskadron Husaren Regiment Nr. 11 and the Ersatz Eskadron of Ulanen Regiment Nr. 5 made up the 4. Mobile Landsturm Eskadron of VII. Armee Korps in August 1914. Scharf painted the Husaren Regiment Nr. 11 Ersatz squadron in their pre-1910 green atilla and black hussar riding breeches. There were two Husar regiments which wore green atillas, the 10th, with yellow facings, and the 11th, which wore white. The strength of the unit was: eight officers, one hundred forty-seven NCOs and troopers, and one hundred sixty-one horses.

A Husar and Wachtmeister of Reserve Husaren Regiment Nr. 8 as they looked on duty in the field, 1914-1915. The Husar carries a zeltbahn rolled over his shoulder and standard Husaren equipment. Scharf notes that the Wachtmeister is wearing a "simplified" uniform and carries a bayonet on his right hip. What is meant by a "simplified" uniform is unclear.

Equipped for action in the field, an Ulan of Westfälisches Ulanen Regiment Nr. 5 mounts a patrol on the Eastern front in 1914. The pear-shaped Ulan-style shoulder boards are piped in white and bear the regimental number sewn in red. The piping of the Ulanka is also in red. The tschapka as worn by the Ulanen is probably the pre-war Model of 1897 as it is shown with a brass articulated chinstrap. It is covered by a cloth cover and carries a black and white Prussian feldzeichen to the front. The equipment is standard light cavalry issue.

A non-commissioned officer of Regiment Jäger zu Pferde Nr. 3. The Jäger zu Pferde regiments were the last cavalry units to be added to the Imperial army. Developed from Meldereiter or field courier units, thirteen regiments were created from 1901 through 1913. The third was established in Colmar in 1903. A special blued metal helmet, M 1905 with a dragoon-style eagle, was issued to all regiments and is seen here under its grey field cover. The uniform was a lighter, almost green feldgrau color; the cuffs and collars bore Kürassier-style decoration, and those of the 3rd were bordered in yellow and green. The regimental number on the shoulder boards is red. The balance of their equipment was standard light cavalry.

A fully equipped Jäger zu Pferde trooper, 1915-1916. In 1915 the helmet was redesigned and designated the M 1915. The trim changed from polished silver or brass to painted grey. Further, articulated brass chinstraps were altered to a more economical leather, as shown here. Scharf points out the equipment consisting of a breadbag, two zeltbahnen or shelter quarters, a gas mask, and a short Kar. 98a.

The Preussen 7. Train Abteilung, August 1914. Train Bataillonen uniforms bore blue piping on the shoulder straps, collars, and cuffs as seen in this painting. As Train transport was basically horse drawn, they were equipped in the style of the cavalry. The Trainsoldat at this early stage of the war still wears pre-1910 black reithose or riding breeches. The helmets are M 1903 pickelhauben with field covers, the swords are specifically for Train troops, and this type was carried by the Prussian, Baden, and Hessian units.

Air warfare of World War I caused a change in the traditional use of artillery. Guns were modified or designed for the purpose of aerial defense and were classified as Flugabwehr-Kanone or Flak. With the advent of night bombing, came the need for searchlights or scheinwerfer to locate the enemy. Therefore, there were Flak Batterien and Scheinwerfer Batterien and the shoulder straps indicated the particular unit. Scharf, in a rather clever manner of showing jackets hung on the line for cleaning, illustrates the design of four Flak variations including the strap for students at the searchlight training school at Hannover. The Gefreite shown wears an M 15 bluse, riding breeches, mounted artillery boots with spurs and a black banded artillery mütze.

Scharf, at his watercolorist's best, paints an officer of II. Baden Grenadier Regiment Kaiser Wilhelm I Nr. 110 in full field equipment, 1914. He is holding the Sabel der Fusstruppen Offiziere in the Baden pattern and it would appear that he was soon to leave for the front.

*A Gefriete and an officer of 9. Badisches "Infanterie Regiment Nr. 170 shown observing the front in
1914. The officer wears a field belt and epaulets of grey cloth instead of silver wire. The Musketier, in
full equipment, has attached his overcoat, zeltbahn and feldmütze to the exterior of his field pack.*

An officer and NCO of Baden Feld-Artillerie Regiment Nr. 30 in field uniforms, 1914. Their ball-topped artillery helmets have cloth field covers with the regimental number applied to the front. The officer is using his brocade dress belt to support his binocular case, holstered P.08, and Prussian model 1904 officer's artillery sword, M 1910. The NCO wears an M 1910 tunic, mounted troops breeches, boots and belt, armed with a P.08 and an enlisted man's nickel-hilted artillery sword M 1874, the scabbards of which were painted black after 1910.

Baden Landsturm troops as they appeared 26 May 1915. The 15. Btl. Vizefeldwebel's M 1910 tunic has plain light blue shoulder straps and NCO gold lace at the cuffs. A covered Landsturm tschako with a Baden yellow and red feldabzeichen, leather gaiters and ID 89 sword are all shown in this painting. The landsturmmann on the right wears an oilcloth-visored cap with the Landsturm cross and the Baden yellow and red cockade. His military appearance is somewhat reduced by the rolled up pant legs and old style side-laced boots. As were most second line troops, he was issued a Gew. 88 and S. 71 bayonet.

An interesting variety of uniforms are shown in this painting of men from the Hessian Infanterie Regiment Grossherzogin (3. Grossherz. Hess) Nr. 117, as were worn in 1915 and 1916. The Oberleutnant on the left with his back to the viewer is wearing a wind jacket as usually identified with mountain troops. The Feldwebel-leutnant wears a privately purchased officer's model uniform of a lightweight cotton material, a schirmmütze with a red and white Hessian cockade, and carries a climbing cane, binoculars and a P. 08. The enlisted men are in M 1910 tunics with the regiment's cipher, crown over "A", on the shoulder straps, covered M 1915 pickelhauben and legwraps with low quarter-laced boots.

Two Musketiere and a Gefreiter of Hessisches Reserve Infanterie Regiment Nr. 222 are portrayed in uniforms worn by the regiment during the hostilities from 1915-1918. On the left the Musketier wears the M 1915 bluse, grey trousers with a thin red stripe and a feldmütze with the Hessian red and white cockade. The man in the center background is wearing a fatigue uniform of grey cotton or "drillich" material. The Gefreiter on the right is wearing an M 1910 tunic with a breadbag strap supporting his M 09 Patronentasche which were dyed black per 1915 regulations. They are all seemingly returning from a most successful mail call.

Two artillery officers as they appeared in 1914. The officer on the left is from the Holstein Feldartillerie Regiment Nr. 24, 3. (Mecklenburg Strelitz) Batterie and is wearing a dress belt complete with sword hangars. The officer on the right is from Grossherzogl. Mecklenburg Feldartillerie Regiment Nr. 60. He is equipped with binoculars and a P. 08 carried on a cavalry-style brown leather belt. Both are carrying the M 1893 Artillerie Offizieren Degan with post-1910 black scabbards.

Scharf's own Jäger Bataillion Nr. 14 in full marching gear as they looked in 1914. The Waldhornist, or French horn musician on the left is wearing the schwalbennester, or swallow's nest shoulder decoration, attached to the uniform with hooks and eyes. The Vizefeldwebel in the center is carrying the tornister or pack of a style unique to Jägers, with a badger skin cover. The feldzeichen on their tschakos were in the colors of Mecklenburg-Schwerin, quartered red and blue on a gold background. Gew. 98s and S.98 bayonets were carried by the Jägers in 1914.

Typical officers of Jäger Bataillion Nr. 14 are shown in this illustration as they served at the front in 1914-1915. The dress bayonets worn by each are of interest, as is the officer's dress belt worn by the Leutnant on the right. Green Jäger piping is in evidence on their tunics and trousers. Scharf calls our attention to the stone grey breeches worn by the man on the left.

*In 1915 men of I. Ersatz-Bataillion, Jäger Bataillion Nr. 14 were still equipped with pre-1910 model
uniforms consisting of dark green waffenrocks and black trousers, both piped in red. The special badger
fur Jäger field pack is shown, as are the Gew. 98 and the early pre-war issue rust-brown breadbag.*

Jäger Bataillion Nr. 14 by 1917 took on the look of troops long engaged in trench warfare. This Jäger is wearing his green banded and piped feldmütze and what Scharf refers to as a Grahenmantel, or trench coat. These were, against orders, shortened and cut down M-15 issue overcoats which made them more practical for wear in the trenches. Often the material removed was cut into strips to make wickelgamaschen, or legwraps. Note the ends of the Bz. 15 hand grenades stacked to the man's right and the M 16 helmet at the ready.

A Hauptmann and Unteroffizier of the Saxon 10. Konigische Sächsisches Infanterie Regiment Nr. 134. The officer has turned back the front and back skirts of his mantel, or overcoat and secured them with the hooks and eyes provided for that purpose which allowed for easier movement when marching. The Unteroffizier is equipped with the M 1894 Mantel für Fussmann-schaften which was later replaced by the field grey Model 1915. Note Scharf shows the Unteroffizier with the field cover turned inside-out, a mistake, or an effort to camouflage the regimental number? Scharf includes the date "1918," but it seems unlikely that much Model 1915 issue would be in evidence by that date.

*Recruits of I. Ersatz-Bataillion, 8. (Konigl. Sachs.) Infanterie Regiment "Prinz Johann Georg" Nr. 107
are illustrated in two types of uniform worn during the training process. The man on the left has been
issued for use during training the old pre-1910 blue uniform with a protective shoulder cover, and grey
drillich cotton trousers. The man on the right is wearing a cotton work jacket, black issue wool trousers
with a red stripe and a protective work apron.*

This trooper, equipped with the special mounted troops mantel or overcoat, is from the Saxon "Karabinier Regiment (2. Schweres Regiment)" on patrol, 1914-1915. His helmet is an M 1893/94 Saxon model of Tomback metal and covered with a grey field cover.

Ulan troopers from the Württemberg Ulan Regiment "König Wilhelm I" Nr. 20. The man in the foreground is wearing an ulanka tunic piped in yellow for the 20th, and the pear-shaped shoulder boards bear the regimental cipher "WI" surmounted by a crown. He is armed with the standard steel lance and a Kavallerie Degen M 89 with the Württemberg state arms on the guard. There were two Württemberg Ulan Regiments, the 19th and the 20th.

A Musketier and officer of 8. Württemberg Infanterie Regiment Nr. 126 "Groscherzog Friedrich von Baden" pose near a pine forest on the Eastern front. The Musketier carries his overcoat rolled over his shelter quarter and is armed with a Gew. 98 and an S. 98 bayonet. The officer's paletot in light grey has a collar of field grey and he carries binoculars and a holstered P. 08 on his officer's field belt. The period is 1914-1915. In this work, we again see Scharf's skills in watercolor.

Uniforms worn from 1914-1916 by officers of Infanterie Regiment "Alt Württemberg" (3. Württembergisch.) Nr. 121. The Hauptmann, on the left, is dressed in the field uniform of 1914 including a field-covered pickelhaube. The Major, in the center, wears a simplified waffenrock, whipcord riding breeches and black riding boots, while the Leutnant (Kompanie Führer) wears the M 15 feldbluse, grey wool riding breeches, officer's schirmmütze, or visored field cap with chinstrap, black boots, brown leather map case and brown support straps for his feldbinde, or service belt.

On the left stands a Kannonier from a Württemberg mountain artillery battery. He has been issued the special mountain tunic with pleated upper pockets and cuff closures, mountain-style reinforced trousers, and a mountain-style cap with fold-down ear flaps, heavy cleated climbing boots and wickelgamasche, or legwraps. Artillerymen were issued Kar. 98a carbines and P. 08 Luger pistols. The Württemberg red and black cockade is on his schneeschuhmütze, or ski cap. The Bavarian Oberleutnant is from the 2.Gebirgs-artillerie Abteilung and wears a short fleece-collared overcoat and a mountain troop cap with a white and blue Bavarian cockade. The period depicted is 1916.

A Major and Kannonier of the 2. Württemberg Feld Artillerie Regiment Nr. 29, "Prinz-Regent Luitpold von Bayern," as they appeared moving to a forward area near the trenches in 1917. The Major wears an officer's field blouse, grey riding breeches, officer's visor schirmmütze with a Württemberg red and black cockade, plus chinstrap and brown leather field equipment. The Kannonier wears the 1910 waffenrock with black artillery piping on the collar and cuffs with the regimental cipher of F. A. 29a "Crown over L." Note the kratschen tucked into the front of his waffenrock.

A Württemberg mountain artillery gunner in full equipment. His ski cap bears a Württemberg red and black cockade on the front and a flaming bomb artillery insignia on the left side. The reinforced mountain troops trousers are tucked into long goat hair stockings which were preferred by most to the wickelgamaschen, or legwraps. The climbing stick is reinforced with a sharp steel end to grip the ice and its handgrip is in the form of a swan's neck. The design of the mountain boot or bergschuh in 1917 was nearly identical to that used in World War II.

An NCO and Musketier of the Bavarian Reserve Infantry Regiment Nr. 8 during the period of 1914-1915. M 1910 uniforms are seen in this painting, as are pickelhauben with field covers or helmüberzüge and the earlier brown leather equipment. The Musketier is armed with a Gew. 88 and the NCO with the Bavarian model artilleriesable or sword. The breadbags and zeltbahn are in a rust brown material, later replaced with material with a hue of field grey color.

On the left of the picture is a Gefreiter of the 2. Bayrisches Fuss-Artillerie Regiment which was garrisoned at Metz. Of interest is the fact that Bavarian artillerymen were issued pickelhauben with pointed spikes rather than the ball-style usually associated with the artillery. This changed in 1916 and all German artillery wore ball-tops on their pickelhauben. The Kannonier on the right is from Rheinisches Fuss Artillerie Regiment Nr. 8 which was also garrisoned at Metz. He is armed with the Kar. 88 carbine with a stacking hook at the muzzle which the cavalry model did not have. A 21 cm mortar nicknamed "Bertha" after Frau Bertha von Krupp und Bohlen-Halbach who, in 1914, was the only living bearer of the famous name of Krupp, may be seen in the background.

Dismounted troopers of 1. (Bayer.) Schweres Reiter Regiment "Prinz Karl von Bayern" clad in white snow camouflage hooded smocks stand guard on the Eastern front in the winter, 1915. By that time more cavalry units were being dismounted and used as infantry.

A trooper of Bavarian Chevaulegers Regiment "Prinz Albrecht v. Preussen" Nr. 6 takes aim with his
Kar. 98a. Following the uniform regulation changes of 1916, the 3rd and the 6th Chavaulegers Regiments
continued to wear uniforms with pink piping as Scharf depicts in this painting.

The Landsturm regiments wore a bewildering variety of uniforms as seen in this picture of two
Landsturmers as they were dressed in 1915. The man on the left has chosen to roll his black overcoat
and wear it on his lower back and fold his zeltbahn and wear it over his shoulder. Both men are in the
issued blue Litewka tunics, one with blue trousers and the other in the more up-to-date feldgrau. The
unit designations were worn on the collar, and in this instance the unit was II Corps, 19th Bataillion.
The Landsturm-style mütze or cap is seen manufactured in grey wool, rather than oilcloth.

More Landsturm uniform variations are seen worn by these Bavarians. The Feldwebel on the left is from Landsturm Infantry Regiment 1 and has been issued the M 1910 uniform with no rank collar button, but with double tressing instead. A black landwehr cross is applied to his pickelhaube field cover and Scharf comments on the old style brown wickelgamaschen legwraps. The man on the left is wearing the same model M 1910 uniform with brown marching boots. His equipment includes a Gew. 88, Patronentasche M 95 cartridge boxes, S. 71 bayonet and an M 1898 spaten or entrenching tool.

A pionier of Bayern Reserve Pionier Komp. 1 is painted by Scharf with full service equipment, or sturmanzug. In evidence are a long-handled handbeil or pionier pick axe and a pionier sawtooth blade S 98/05 bayonet which is distinguished by its wide scabbard. His kratschen or mütze carries a black band piped in red the same as found on the caps of artillery and other verkherstruppen.

Scharf does not specifically identify these troops, but from all appearances the two in the left and right positions are on a work detail. The man on the left wears an M 1910 tunic under a cotton work or fatigue jacket and a mütze with a black band. The center figure is wearing a visor cap, schirmmütze M 1912, usually associated with motorized troops, and a grey Litewka. The man on the right man is wearing a grey cotton drillich jacket, NCO visor cap with a red band, and feldgrau trousers. His eyeglasses look to be the type worn under the gas mask which is slung from the shoulders of all three.

Guard duty in 1916 is being performed by an Ulan of the 2. Bayerisches Ulanen Regiment "König."
The Bavarians fielded two Ulan regiments whose facing colors were a red-maroon, as can be seen in
this painting. The pear-shaped shoulder boards bear the regimental number "2" and his mütze bears
the white and blue cockade of Bavaria. Reinforced riding breeches and black cavalry-style boots complete
his uniform. His weapon is a Kar. 98a and the background has a decidedly Eastern front look.

In May 1916, a Musketier of the 12. (Bayer) Infanterie Regiment "Prinz Arnulf" stands ready to repel an attack. His M 1910 tunic has Swedish-style cuffs and the shoulder straps bear his regimental numbers. His equipment includes an assault pack, a gas mask, two canteens, an ersatz bayonet with a grey-painted hilt, a Gew. 98, and black marching boots with leather tighteners at the ankles.

On the left, Scharf depicts a member of Bayern Reserve Infanterie Regiment Nr. 19 equipped for an assault. He is wearing a modified M 1910 tunic with buttoned straps on the sleeves, blue-grey trousers and field grey legwraps. He is equipped with an assault pack, gas mask, ammunition bandolier, a Gew. 98 and an M 16 helmet. On the right is a member of Ersatz Infanterie Regiment Nr. 5 who is still wearing an M 1915 pickelhaube with field cover, as late as 22 July 1916. Of interest is a grey enameled canteen hung from his canvas breadbag.

A cyclist of the Bavarian Radfahr-Bataillion Nr. 3 as he appeared on the Eastern front, December 1916. He is wearing an M 1915 tschako with a field cover and a blue and white feldzeichen; also, an M 1910 tunic with green Jäger piping, steel grey trousers, field grey legwraps and front-laced low-quarter boots. Scharf shows this Radfahr man armed with a standard Gew. 98, not with the bicycle troops model with turned down bolt and side-mounted sling.

By 1918 most mounted troops were fighting on the ground, but a few in special units still retained their mounts. Here is seen a trooper of the Bavarian 1. Schweres Reiter Regiment "Prinz Karl v. Bayern" wearing the Bavarian M 1916 bluse with blue and white collar tressing and yellow and blue shoulder straps. Also of interest is his M 1918 steel helmet with the cutout brim. All the horse equipment is standard cavalry issue, as are the Kar. 98a carbines and steel lances.

Scharf's exposure to the Eastern front and the Czarist Russians encountered there inspired him to add a few Russian images to the Zweierlei Tuch collection. On the left is an officer of the 9th Dragoon Regiment in his winter field uniform. His shoulder boards bear "9" for his regiment and he is armed with a holstered seven-shot Nagant M 1895 revolver of 7.62 mm caliber and M 1881 Dragoon pattern "shashka" saber. On the right is an officer of the 4th Dragoon Regiment in the summer service uniform similarly armed.

In this watercolor Scharf illustrates two officers dressed in winter parade uniforms from 1914. On the left, the officer of the 13th Dragoons is wearing a late version of the "Patemkin" helmet of an early nineteenth century design, which was re-introduced in 1854 at the time of the Crimean War. All but three Dragoon regiments wore this style helmet with either white or black crest decoration, and a Russian Imperial eagle plate in the front. The 13th was the only regiment with the diamond-shaped plate. The 16th, 17th, and 18th Dragoons wore a red cloth skull cap bound in black astrakhan fur with a Russian Imperial eagle attached to the front as shown in the right hand figure.

6. Dragoner Regiment
"Gluchow"
J.H.H. der Großfürstin
Alexandra Josefowna
Winterparadeuniform in der front.

offizier
vom

18. Dragoner Regiment
"Ssewersk"
des Königs Christian IX.
von Dänemark.
Winterparadeuniform in der front.

Dragoon officers from the 6th and 18th Dragoon Regiments in winter service uniforms. The 16th, 17th, and 18th Dragoons carried Cossack-style "shashka" swords which had no hand guard and a distinctive shaped grip, while the other units, as seen here, carried the M 1881 Dragoon pattern.

13. Dragoner Regiment
"Kriegsorden"
des Generalfeldmarschalls
Grafen Münnich.
Paradeuniform in der Front.

Offizier von

5. Dragoner Regiment
"Kargopol."
Paradeuniform außer der
Front.

Officers of the 13th and 5th Dragoons in summer parade uniforms as were worn at the front in 1914.
The tunics were of lightweight wool or cotton duck material.

14. Dragoner Regiment
„Kleinrussland"
des Kronprinzen des deutschen
Reiches und von Preußen,
Paradeuniform außer der Front.

Offizier
von

7. Dragoner Regiment
„Kinburn".
gewöhnliche Uniform
außer der Front.

Officers of the 14th and 7th Dragoon Regiments. The officer on the left is in parade dress; the officer on the right is in the walking-out dress uniform.

RUSSLAND.

SOMMER - UND DIENSTUNIFORMEN

PARADEUNIFORMEN

IN·DER·FRONT.

AUSSER·DER·FRONT.

HIER·DRAGONER·REGT.4 UND 7. OFFIZIERE.

87.

Officers of the 4th and 7th Dragoons in parade uniform. Note that in these paintings of Russians each Dragoon regiment had a distinctive color combination to their caps. Scharf describes the parade uniform on the left as worn at the front, and the one the right as worn away from the front.

11. Dragoner Regiment
„Riga"
Winterdienstuniform
(Halbpelz).

Offizier
vom

12. Dragoner Regiment
„Starodub"
Dienstuniform außer
der Front.

On the left is an 11th Dragoon officer dressed in a winter mounted patrol jacket edged in astrakhan fur, riding breeches, boots with spurs, and holding a riding crop. The officer of the 12th is in the service uniform not worn at the front.

15. Dragoner Regiment
„Perejaslawl"
Kaiser Alexander III.
Winterparadeuniform
in der front . (mit Epauletten)

Offizier
vom

13. Dragoner Regiment
„Kriegsorden"
des Generalfeldmarschalls
Grafen Münnich.
Winter- Paradeuniform außer der front,

Officers of the 15th and 13th Dragoon Regiments in their winter parade uniforms. The 13th, as well as wearing a distinctive helmet plate, wore a dress uniform of dark blue, trimmed much like the uniform of the Prussian Kürassier Regiments. The officer of the 15th is in the parade uniform as seen at the front, while the 13th Officer is dressed for parade away from the front.

Also from the Publisher